IMAGES
of England

GORTON
THE SECOND SELECTION

Members of the Gore Street mission chapel 9th Gorton Girl Guide and Brownie companies take part in the Whit Walks in the 1950s. They are on Church (later Cambert) Lane, with banner bearer Linda McGuirk. Behind them is the banner of the Wellington Street Primitive Methodist chapel Sunday school. This chapel, purchased from the Baptists, began life in 1874 and closed in 1958.

Front cover: King George V Silver Jubilee party in Henry Street, West Gorton, 1935. (Photograph kindly loaned by Reg Baguley.)

IMAGES
of England

GORTON
THE SECOND SELECTION

Jill Cronin and Frank Rhodes

TEMPUS

To the late Alan Aikin,
an evacuee with fond memories of East Manchester

Reddish Lane, Gorton, in the early 1900s. On the right is Aspinall (or Aspinal) Wesleyan Methodist church. This is the second church, built in 1877, and superseded in 1910 by the 'Centenary' church, which would replace these cottages on the right and itself be replaced in 1972 by a smaller church. On the right also lies Brook Green House near Turnbull Road and opposite were householders and a smallware dealer.

First published 2002, reprinted 2004.

Tempus Publishing Limited
The Mill, Brimscombe Port,
Stroud, Gloucestershire, GL5 2QG
www.tempus-publishing.com

British Library Cataloguing in Publication Data.
A catalogue record for this book is available from the British Library.

ISBN 0 7524 2669 9

Typesetting and origination by Tempus Publishing Limited.
Printed in Great Britain.

Contents

'Save Mellands Field'. Residents campaigned to save this piece of open space near their homes on Wembley Road in July 1975. From the left, standing, are Ethel Rhodes and Mrs Eyres, Mrs McGrath, Mrs Tidsey and Mrs Smith. These playing fields, bounded by Melland, Mount and Wembley Roads and Sandfold Lane, after public fundraising, were opened in 1907 by Ald. William Melland, chairman of the Manchester and Salford Playing Fields Society. During the Second World War there was a military police army camp on the Wembley Road side for Italian prisoners of war.

Introduction

Since the first selection of photographs of Gorton appeared in 1998, we have been amazed by the number of people who have made contact from all over Manchester, further afield and abroad, who originate from Gorton. During the clearances of the 1970s and 1980s rows of housing and shops were swept away and countless people, having lost their homes and livelihood, moved away. There is nostalgia for Gorton past and especially for Gorton Monastery.

When we came to compile this second selection, as well as using the remaining few photographs from the collection of the late Stan Horritt, we were loaned fascinating family photographs illustrating families in Gorton, at school, at work, on the Whit Walks, getting married or just standing outside their homes in a street that no longer exists.

It is hard to believe now that Gorton started life as a country village, straggling the valley of the Gore Brook, stretching westwards towards Ardwick and the city of Manchester and eastwards to the wooded area of Debdale Vale. The farms and fields of those days were soon covered by the explosion of industry that hit Gorton and by the housing needed for the workforce. Few signs of farming remain: one such is Spring Hill (or Bank) farmhouse off Tan Yard Brow and now a cattery and kennels.

West Gorton and Gorton were one until 1890, when the city of Manchester took over the former, as they would also eventually consume Gorton. Rows and rows of terraced housing were swept away and now it is hard to imagine how densely populated the town was. As most streets had their names changed, it is even more difficult to place the roads.

People need work, housing, services and shops. Gorton had industries to be proud of, many of them straggled the town's border with Openshaw. Crossley Motors, Gorton Tank, Beyer Peacock, Vaughan's Cranes, Armstrong Whitworth, and Kendall & Gent were household names. The rows of small shops that lined the main routes have also been cleared away. It is hard to visualise the bustling scenes along Hyde Road, Gorton Lane and Cross (later Gorton-cross) and Wellington Streets. Larger houses too have also suffered. Long gone are Gorton Hall and High Bank, and Kenyon, Gorton and Gorton Brook Houses. Recently, the row of elegant houses along Hyde Road, opposite Debdale Park, was demolished to be replaced by apartments. Only one survives of these homes, the hat masters of Denton. One success story was back in 1971, when a public outcry saved the tan yard workers' cottages on Tan Yard Brow.

A town needs public buildings, public houses, places of entertainment, churches and schools. So far Gorton has lost its town hall near Belle Vue and its libraries at West Gorton as well as the old Gorton Library on Church (later Cambert) Lane. Now its swimming pool at Gorton

Tub has closed, in spite of public opposition. Gorton probably did have almost 'a pub on every corner': working in industry was thirsty work. Many of these have long gone and more closed in recent times as trends in drinking changed but the Gorton Arms came to the most unexpected closure recently, after a collision with a JCB. Two public houses, owned by the Jennison family of Belle Vue, have closed: the Midland is empty and the Lake Hotel demolished. The Plough Inn is one of the few to remain unchanged with its original fittings and cobbled front yard.

None of the old cinemas still operate, such as the Corona, Cosmo, Savoy, Plaza, Essoldo and Olympia, but the Showcase cinema complex has replaced them. The Belle Vue Zoological and Pleasure Gardens were known nationally, attracting thousands of visitors and employing hundreds locally. Belle Vue is not represented in this selection but is the subject of another book in this series.

Numerous churches have disappeared, including St Mark's, All Saints' and most of the Methodist and Baptist chapels. Trinity Baptist on Wellington Street, recently demolished, is to be rebuilt and Gorton Monastery restored. At least the two successors of the original Gorton Chapels remain, St James's replacing the Anglican and Brookfield the Independent chapels. Many church schools have closed too, as well as some of the state ones. Only recently Spurley Hey secondary and Ellen Wilkinson at Ardwick were replaced by Cedar Mount high school.

Looking at photographs of Whit Walks, VE Day parties, May and Rose Queens, the Rush Cart ceremony and other community events, it is no surprise that the community spirit lives on in Gorton. Neighbourhood groups abound to improve the area. Gorton is also attracting hotel and leisure developments. Gorton Local History group compiles memories and records of the area, as well as publishing books.

Gorton Heritage action group has greatly improved the Gore Brook Valley conservation area, including a published trail, wildflower meadow and now a butterfly garden. Melland's playing fields were saved back in the 1970s. The future of Debdale Vale, with its reservoirs, park and golf courses, is still uncertain, as the planned development, called Waterside Park and originally Kingswater, threatens to erode another 'green lung' of Gorton, Denton and Audenshaw.

Perhaps the most pleasing news of all is the success of the Friends of Gorton Monastery in saving this fine building and friary complex of St Francis of Assisi for Gorton. Designed by Edward Welby Pugin, a son of Augustus Pugin, and home to the Franciscan monks since 1861, it has lain derelict since they departed in 1989. Its tall spire is an important and distinctive landmark in the town. After restoration, it is hoped to have a museum of East Manchester there, where Belle Vue memorabilia will have pride of place. This project should aid regeneration, along with other conservation and neighbourhood projects. We hope that this selection of photographs will help to remind people of what Gorton has looked like in the past and where to find traces of its heritage.

One
Steet Scenes

Two ladies trudge up Ryder Brow off Far Lane in the 1970s. At the top of the hill was Ryder's Fold with a row of cottages leading to Ryder Brow school (see pp 82-5). In the 1920s the Ryder Brow council estate was built, stretching across to Gorton cemetery. The foot of the hill, known as 'Bottom 'o' th' Brow' and Winning (or Winding) Hill, was by legend the site of a battle against the Danes. Nearby lie two gravestones belonging to yeoman farmer James (1826-1890) and Sarah (1816-1877) Barlow of Levenshulme.

Looking eastwards along Hyde Road towards Gorton bridge, *c.* 1915. On the right is Brookfield Sunday school, now converted into apartments, and beyond it is the spire of Brookfield Unitarian church, which, when opened in 1871, replaced the Dissenting or Independent Gorton chapel of 1703 off Far Lane. The old burial ground adjoins the newer one by the Gore Brook and contains memorials to many well known and influential local people.

Looking north from Hyde Road along Wellington Street to its junction with Cross Lane and Gortoncross (late Cross) Street, 1973. Most of these shops have now gone and so has the Baptist chapel (a rebuilding plan is on the way) just out of view on the right. Garlick Street turns off first right with the former Manchester and County Bank building on its near corner. In the distance Jessop (late John) Street turns off right. On the left lies the former Cosmo cinema by Duke Street, with Gorton Terrace, Hopefield (late Hope) and Banville (late Bank) Streets leading off to the left.

Gortoncross (late Cross) Street looking south-west towards Hyde Road, 1974. This main area for shopping was mostly cleared for a new shopping centre in 1980. From the right are the Bargain Shop, Direct Fish Supplies, the Biscuit Shop and the double-fronted Lancashire Hygienic Dairies (there in 1910). In the 1960s Price the baker's, Murphy's fishmonger's and Love furnisher's, next to Whalley Street, followed on. Opposite was the Rose and Crown public house.

Gortoncross Street looking north-east towards its junction with Wellington Street and continuing as Cross Lane, where on the left of the lane used to stand Wellington Street Primitive Methodist chapel. From the left in the 1960s were Melia's grocer's shop, Harlin's opticians and Ray's dress shop, still there in the 1970s. Opposite the shops lay the Rose of England public house (see p.111) and Gore (later Gorelan) Street.

11

Gortoncross Street looking south-west towards Hyde Road, near to Wellington Street, 1974. The fruit shop on the right is in the previous picture and shows the continuing line of shops, which also went in the clearances of 1980. In the 1960s this double-fronted shop was Melia's grocery, followed by Parker's butcher's, Manstyle outfitter's, Johnson Bros dyer's, a boot and shoe dealer, Vernon's grocery, a butcher's shop and Sutcliffe's provision dealers. Here in 1910 was the Maypole dairy.

Gortoncross Street looking from the Hyde Road end north-east towards Wellington Street, 1973. The Manchester and Salford Trustee savings bank is in this row on the right. In 1910 there were a chemist, china, boot, fried fish, clothes, butcher's, and furniture shops and dining rooms in this row.

12

Cross (later Gortoncross) Street looking south-west towards Hyde Road from Wellington Street, 1908. On the left in the 1960s lay Bell's china and Ward's butcher's shop, followed by the Rose of England public house (see p.111) here on the corner of Gore (later Gorelan) Street, with Henry Hyde's grocery on its opposite corner. Among the shops on the right lay Lipton's grocery, Moore's bird dealer, Watson's greengrocery and the Liverpool Meat Co. butchers store with Whalley Street beyond.

Hyde Road looking east towards Denton, in the 1920s. Off the picture right lies the Midland public house. Next comes Belle Vue station by Station (later Glencastle) Road, convenient for one of the entrances to Belle Vue pleasure gardens by the Lake Hotel (see p.17, 115). In the background of the station is visible the Chatsworth mill of Robert Williams & Sons, silk finishers. On the left most of the shops lining Hyde Road were cleared in the 1980s.

Hyde Road looking west towards Belle Vue and Manchester, c. 1917. On the left is the Midland Hotel with the wall of the Corporation works yard leading to the tower of Gorton town hall, with the Lake Hotel across Kirkmanshulme Lane in the distance. On the right is a line of shops, now all gone, by Church (later Cambert) Lane, on whose far corner is the Empire grocery stores with Mark Hall beerseller (the Three Arrows public house) opposite. On the far right in the distance is the tower of Gorton public baths on the corner of Queen's Road.

Hyde Rd, Gorton

Hyde Road looking west towards Belle Vue, around 1917. On the left is the turning into Kirkmanshulme Lane with the Lake Hotel (see p.115) and the perimeter wall of Belle Vue beyond. On the right is the Empire grocery stores on the corner of Church Lane, which was the grocery of Benjamin Greenfield in 1899, Nathaniel Gould by 1908, George Ward in 1910 and by the 1960s Sharples' bakery. The row of shops included in 1908 Manchester corporation tramways office, a confectioner, fruiterer, draper and the Post Office bank.

Opposite below: The 'Ten Houses' or 'Pink Bank Cottages' on the east side of Mount Road in the 1970s. Now demolished, these houses stood on the corner of Melland Road (late Pink Bank Lane) on a field line. Behind them stretched fields, until the Mount Road estate and allotments were built in the 1920s, covering the fields and extending the unadopted cart track of Mount Road.

Another view of Hyde Road looking west near Belle Vue in the late 1930s. On the left is the Lake Hotel with a horse trough in front and on the right George Mason's grocery store on the corner of Church Lane, where the Empire grocery stores had stood earlier.

Hyde Road by the entrance to Belle Vue on the left off Kirkmanshulme Lane, around 1915. The tram is travelling eastwards towards Denton. On the right is the grocery stores on the corner of Church Lane. Mount Road just off Kirkmanshulme Lane was the terminus for Belle Vue in the 1920s and 1930s. The tramcars turned right at the Lake Hotel and then left to travel round Gorton town hall and so left again back to Piccadilly in the city.

The entrance to Belle Vue pleasure gardens and zoo off Kirkmanshulme Lane, with Hyde Road in the background in the 1920s. This was known as the East, Gorton or Lake entrance, as it adjoined the Lake Hotel on the right. Both hotel and entrance were opened in 1876 for visitors via nearby Belle Vue station. Other entrances were on Hyde Road, at Longsight and on Redgate Lane.

Belle Vue junction in the 1960s. Kirkmanshulme Lane and Mount Road join with Hyde Road in the distance. The Lake Hotel on the left carries an advertisement for a boxing match between Cullen and Grant. On the right is Gorton town hall with Price's bakery in the far row of shops, where a Redfern's lorry turns the corner.

Queen's Road on the left off the north side of Hyde Road, 1973. In the 1960s from the left the travel agency was still there, next to an outfitter, double-fronted drapery, boot and shoe dealer, newsagent and men's outfitters on the corner of Mona (late Edward) Street. Queen's Road leads to Gorton Lane and on its opposite corner stands Gorton public baths (see p.42).

The railway bridge running over Ryder Brow Road with Dean Road leading left, in the 1950s. It is viewed from Woodland Avenue, which continues over to meet Alexandra (later Alvaston) Road on the edge of Gorton public cemetery. The railway line travels south-west to Levenshulme South station and north to Gorton's Hyde Road and Fairfield stations.

Birch Street curving round into Brunswick (late Blackwin) Street up to Gorton Monastery in the distance, 1991. This area has changed through street clearances. On the right is the site of Birch Street Baptist chapel next to Corby Street. Opened in 1880, after a move from Ainsworth Street (built 1878) this chapel was closed in the 1970s, combining with Wellington Street chapel. The next turning off Birch Street on the right is Belle Vue Street with Birch Street running down on the right to Hyde Road.

Birch Street leading up to Hyde Road in the distance, where the flags fly of British Car Auctions, 1991. On the left lies Great Jones Street with the site of Birch Street Baptist chapel on the far left bounded by Brunswick (late Blackwin) Street. On the right is Feltham (late New) Street, with beyond it the Imperial Inn, once with its own brewery (see p.59). Behind the houses on the left stretched the large Globe iron works.

Clowes Street, West Gorton, looking north-east towards West Gorton library, in the early 1900s. The library lay on the junction of Belle Vue and Clowes Streets and Gorton Lane. Shops line Clowes Street. On the right is an array of streets, including Gladstone and Norton and on the left Arthur and Jane, plus the Queen's public house.

Two

Out of Doors

Barbara Taylor with Wilfred Price and her young sister and brother, Christine and David Taylor, in the 1950s. They are standing in Gorton Park with Queen's Road behind them and Hyde Road in front of them. Opened in 1893 by Gorton urban district council, this park was acquired by Manchester corporation along with Gorton's other parks.

Gorton Upper reservoir viewed from the recreation ground at Abbey Hey (see p.24) in the early 1900s. This area was known as Debdale Vale and this reservoir along with Gorton Lower was one of the first two reservoirs for the area in 1826. Manchester and Salford waterworks went on later to open Denton and Audenshaw reservoirs adjoining Gorton's. Manchester corporation took them over in 1851 and then North West Water authority, now United Utilities.

Gorton Upper reservoir viewed from Debdale park, in the 1960s. To the left is the Lower reservoir. This park, opened in 1912, covers the south-west corner of Debdale Vale.

A FAVOURITE WALK GORTON RESERVOIR

The 'Favourite Walk' between the Gorton reservoirs, 1905. The walled walk, running between the Upper on the left and the Lower on the right, was officially called Green Fold and is viewed here from Abbey Hey looking towards Gorton. It separated Abbey Hey sports ground from Abbey Hey recreation ground and then separated the reservoirs, passing eventually through Debdale Park and onto Hyde Road.

Barbara Taylor standing in Gorton Park in the 1950s. Barbara lived in Saighton Street at that time with her family, including her sisters Elsie and Christine and her brother David (see pp 21,45-46). This park also possessed a bandstand, two bowling greens, pavilion, two tennis courts, a rest garden and children's play area. The park contained more recreational than floral elements.

ABBEY HEY RECREATION GROUND, GORTON.

Abbey Hey recreation ground, 1918. This was south-west of Fairfield golf course in the grounds of Abbeyfield house. There were also Abbey Hey playing fields north-west of the golf course off Violet and Coram Streets and the King George VI playing fields, opened in 1950 off Chapman Street. These recreation grounds were opened in 1909 between High Bank and Green Fold and later became a park. Abbey Hey gardens, opened in 1869, lay off Abbey Hey Lane by the railway and Hodson (later Vine) Street, but closed in 1893 for housing.

Elsie Slockett (née Taylor) sitting by the side of Debdale weir near Debdale Park at Gorton reservoir in the 1960s. The park with its 48.5 acres included rose and other flower gardens. By the 1970s there were many amenities, including a bandstand, miniature golf course (9 holes for 10p), two bowling greens (4p an hour), nine tennis courts (20p an hour), six football pitches, a rest shelter and a pets' corner. Fishing rights in the reservoir cost 20p a day for coarse fishing and 30p for trout. Each summer a pleasure fair still comes to the park.

Farm buildings on Levenshulme Road opposite Lowfell Walk, prior to demolition in 1985. Gorton originally relied on farming and numerous farms covered the attractive Gore Brook valley and area centred on Gorton village. Few survive now as industry took over very early on. Spring Hill (or Bank) farm, built around 1780, off Tan Yard Lane is one of the few left, being now a kennels and cattery.

Farm buildings on Levenshulme Road prior to demolition in 1985. This farm became a dyeworks. Other farms were Lower and Higher Catsknowl by Belle Vue, Mount off Mount Road, Sunny Brow, Ashton Fold near the Plough Inn, Rylands and Chapel farms.

Colin Southworth in Sunny Brow park, 1954. Behind him lies Levenshulme Road with a path off to the right leading to the bridge over the Gore Brook, which traverses this linear park. In the background on the left are St Philip's church and housing on St Philip's Road.

Sunny Brow park with the spire of Brookfield Unitarian church in the distance, in the 1960s. Opened in 1905 and named from a forty-five acre farm on the site, this park was declared a Conservation Area in 1995. It stretches from west to east, divided lengthwise by the Gore Brook and ending at Maiden's Bridge. The park is bounded by Brook, Knutsford and Haworth Roads and Hall (later Hengist) Street.

Sunny Brow park around 1910. The children stand near the bridge over the Gore Brook and behind them is Brookfield Unitarian church and Haworth Road, bordering the north side of the park. The original valley of the brook forms the park, as it nestles between two main roads, Hyde Road and Reddish Lane. The original Gorton village lay nearby, stretching from here northwards to Gorton Chapel, the forerunner of St James's church (see pp. 68-70).

High Bank Park in the late 1920s. This park was opened as recreation grounds in 1909 on the site of High Bank House off High Bank. This house, now demolished, was home to the Grimshaw family in the late 1700s until the 1840s, when a different Grimshaw family moved in until the late 1890s. The Grimshaws had other houses locally and were big employers in the area.

Three
People and Places

Members of St James's church taking part in the Whit Walks in the 1950s. Centre front, facing the camera, is Sheila Moore. They are passing Gore Street post office, which was demolished in the 1970s during the clearances along Hyde Road. This was on the corner of Gore (later Gorelan) Street, opposite a surgeon's house. There was a post master, James Turner, in 1833 near the Plough Inn on Hyde Road.

Houses on the south side of Hyde Road, 1990. These grand homes on the border of Denton and Gorton, opposite Debdale Park, became fashionable for wealthier families, after the construction of Manchester/Hyde Road in 1818. On the right is Glentyan House, the only survivor, on the east corner of Brighton Range and inhabited mostly by doctors since 1910. On the left is Cambridge House, home to the Oldham family of Oldham Batteries and later divided into two properties.

On the right is the row of houses on the east corner of Claremont Range, Hyde Road, 1990. Between Westbourne and Claremont Ranges lay three police houses, Highfield Range and Edenagreena House, where the Woolfendens, a hatting family, lived. Next came Carlton Range and then Carlton House,where the Moores and later the Howes lived. There were three houses in this row, Eskdale, Oakleigh and Westwood, ending at Delahays Range. On the left is Westwood on the west corner of Delahays (late Beech) Range.

On the right is the row of six houses on Hyde Road on the east side of Delahays Range, 1990. The first three from the right were Lonsdale, Glenside and Dovestone, while the next three were Heathfield, Hollybank and Fair Holme. On the left is Fair Holme, the last house on this row.

Opposite below: Abington House on Hyde Road, 1990. This area was once the site of Highfield House and the fields of Mount Pleasant Farm. Now all the houses, except Glentyan, have been demolished and apartments built on the land. Abington, on the west corner of Westbourne Range and adjoining Cambridge and Glentyan Houses, was home to Amos Hill a builder in 1910.

On the right is a house on the border of Gorton and Denton on Hyde Road, 1990. On the left is the last row of houses in Gorton on Hyde Road near Laburnum Road, with Denton to the left. There were five cottages, which included a confectioner, dressmaker and boot repairer.

The entrance gates to Gorton public cemetery in the 1950s. Behind them lie the Non-Conformist, Church of England and Roman Catholic chapels. The cemetery was opened in 1900 by Hugh Dean for Gorton urban district council and was enclosed by two railway lines, the Manchester and Ashton canal and Alvaston (late Alexandra Road).

Above: Paupers' graves in Gorton public cemetery. The cemetery contains many interesting memorials to important and well-known local personalities, but this poignant row in a corner of the cemetery reminds us that not only the rich and well known are buried here.

Right: The memorial in Gorton public cemetery to those employees at Belle Vue pleasure gardens, who died following action in the First World War. Set up in 1926 by the Jennison family and unveiled by Angelo Jennison, the memorial's nineteen names included two Jennisons. Long serving family names are also inscribed such as Craythorne. The intricate carving adorning the top of the memorial has sadly been lost.

Mrs Doreen Merron stands on the left, along with Mr and Mrs Arthur Calvert and Mrs Emily Alker at the doors of their cottages on the east side of Tan Yard Lane, 1971. Tanner's Row was home to workers in the nearby tannery on Tan Yard Brow over the bridge by the Gore Brook. Leather was important locally in the hat making trade.

The rear of the cottages on Tan Yard Lane, 1998. These cottages for the tannery workers are two-storied at the front and three-storied at the back. There are two rows of cottages, one behind the other with Tanners' Street. Three thousand people signed a petition to save these houses, when they were declared unfit in the 1970s, and so they still survive to this day.

Above: The row of four cottages on the west side of High Bank, just below Hobart (late Melbourne) Street, 1998. Spring Hill (or Bank) farm lies just below them on the left. One huge piece of wood called the King beam runs through the whole row.

Right: Demolition of cottages on Far Lane, 1980. There were about twenty cottages along this lane on the same side as the Lollipop shop. In the distance is Hyde Road and a garage near the Waggon and Horses public house. Behind the chimney of the cottage is the spire of Brookfield Unitarian church, which is also on Hyde Road.

The front entrance to Gorton Hall in 1890. This was not the original hall, where the Gorton family first lived close to Gorton village from around 1681. John Gorton had this new hall built in 1715 and Richard Peacock of the firm Beyer Peacock & Co. (see pp 60-62) was to live there from the early 1860s. This building was demolished but one of its three lodges still stands off Old Hall Drive and Brookhurst Road. This is the Front lodge; the Yard and Back ones have gone.

A stone plaque on the wall of a house on Park Terrace on Brookhurst Road. This commemorates the site of Gorton Hall and bears the initials 'W.H.W'. and the date 1906, after the hall was demolished and these houses built. On the wall bounding the front garden an inscription also reads 'W.H.W. 1906': presumably these initials belong to the architect or builder of the houses.

Houses on Hyde Road opposite Far Lane and the Waggon and Horses public house in the 1980s. Now demolished, there were four houses on the corner of the dirt track on the left, which led to Fox Fold over the Gore Brook. In 1908 the first two were occupied by William Howard & Sons drysalters at Sunnyside works. The third was lived in by an oil refiner and the last on the right by a schoolmaster.

Two houses, now demolished, off the dirt track leading to Kirk Street, left, and Fox Fold across the Gore Brook and so to Croft Bank, 1964. The name plate on the houses reads 'Sunny Side'.

One of the cottages on 'Briton's (or Britton's) Row', now demolished, 1973. These were built in 1782 by Joseph Taylor and stood near Kirk Lane and the Vale Cottage public house (see p.111). Joseph, who died in 1800, used to declare when drunk, 'I am a Briton' and the nickname stuck.

A view of the rear of a cottage on 'Briton's Row', 1973. The row was dog-legged in shape and lay behind Croft Bank. An extra cottage was added in 1849 but all have now been demolished.

A row of houses on Hyde Road on the corner of Chapman Street, 2001. Of these houses, built around 1880, the first, called The Oaks, was inhabited in 1908 by the Revd Cunningham of the Wesleyan church, next to One Ash, Ivy Villa and Brookfield on the right. In the 1960s the first two houses were inhabited by dentists and the last on the right by an undertaker's, where in 1891 Peter Hindle, clerk to the Local Board, lived.

Kenyon House, now demolished, on Wellington Street, 1973. Named after the landowner, Lord Kenyon, it was built in about 1880 for John Buckley (1834-1916), son of John the owner of Buckley's Gorton New Mill, from whom he took over. In 1881 he is described as a 'cotton manufacturer and brewer' with a workforce of 260. Nicknamed 'Gorton's millionaire', he also endowed Gorton's free library in 1900 as his gift to the people of Gorton. The library is now demolished.

A house, now demolished, on Cambert (late Church) Lane, 1970. It is said that stone from Belle Vue prison was used in its construction. The clay used to make the bricks for the prison was extracted from the prison site. Many homes in the area boast of materials from Belle Vue prison or from the pleasure gardens. One family has a drive made up of paving from the elephant house.

Some of the prison warders' houses on Forbes Street off Hunter's Lane, prior to demolition in the early 1970s. These were close to Belle Vue prison, which in turn was next to Belle Vue pleasure gardens and zoo. On the right is the stadium of Belle Vue Speedway.

The rear of some of the prison warders' houses on Hyde Road, prior to demolition, in the early 1970s. They stood near Belle Vue and are viewed from Hunter's Lane. Washhouses stood at the back here and indoors they had Lancashire ranges.

Belle Vue borough prison on Hyde Road in the early 1880s. Opened on the former Gorton Brook estate in 1850, the prison lay alongside Belle Vue pleasure gardens until demolition in1890. Cells and tunnels from the prison were said to lie under the pleasure garden site. Front left lies the bowling green of the Coach and Horses public house.

Another view of Belle Vue prison, which was also nicknamed 'Nutsford Gaol', because it lay in Nutsford Vale. The prison housed 451 men and women in 1851, but by 1886 the Prison Commissioners had closed it down.

Gorton washhouse and public baths off Hyde Road on the corner of Queen's Road, 1984. Men and women entered by separate doorways, the women entering by the left-hand door. Opened in 1890 these baths provided facilities for swimming and washing, as well as for laundry and washing clothes. The building escaped demolition and has found a new role as an Institute of Gymnastics.

Brook House flats, West Gorton, at the junction of Gorton Lane and Belle Vue and Clowes Streets, in the 1960s. The Yorkshire Hotel previously stood on the site and during the Second World War the four-storey flats were started but completed later.

The inner courtyard of Brook House flats, derelict prior to demolition, in the late 1970s. The centre archway led through to Gorton Lane where rows of shops stood opposite. The site was originally covered by Gorton Brook House with the Corn Brook flowing just north of it. Brookhouse Road behind the flats also recalled this name.

Above: Tracy Reynolds standing on her father's Ford Consul car outside one of the entrances to Brook House flats in the 1950s.

Left: Mrs Baguley stands by the Paddock in Belle Vue Zoo, 1959. Behind her is Greenwood House on Kirkmanshulme Lane at its junction with Pink Bank Lane. These flats were demolished in the 1980s.

Barbara Taylor with her younger sister Elsie outside their home on Little Nelson Street, 1937. They were about to move to their first house in Gorton on Far Lane.

Barbara Taylor with her youngest sister Christine standing outside their next home, in the 1950s. Home was No. 6 Saighton Street, which lay off Queen's Road at the side of Gorton public baths.

Ronnie Hawkes, aged eleven, stands behind twins Pat (on the left) and Brenda Beaumont with baby brothers Fred and Frank (at the front) Torr, 1949. All were related and are outside one of the family homes at No.10, Deepdene (late Hampden) Street, which ran off Hyde Road to Great Jackson Street, West Gorton. Nearby was the Harrington public house.

The three sisters, Barbara, Christine and Elsie Taylor on the right outside No. 32, Hexham Road, 1954. They also had a brother called David (see p.21). This road lay off East Road, off Mount Road.

Above: Susan and Marion, nieces of Reg Baguley, stand on Henry (later Beaumaris) Street, 1958. In the distance is Clowes Street and to the right Watson Street.

Left: Robert Rhodes, Frank's brother, aged three months, with his aunt Joan Morris (née Statham), 1945. Joan was sister to their mother Ethel. They are outside their mother's home at No. 10, Cleadon Avenue, on the estate between Mount Road and the station.

The Heap family of Gorton Lane, 1913. In the back row from the left are Samuel Heap (Lancashire Fusilier), Ernest Rhodes and Joseph Heap, head of the family. At the front on the left sits Joseph's daughter, who is Ernest's wife, Annie Rhodes (née Heap) with her baby son Frank. Next to her stands young Victor Heap (nicknamed 'George'), then Mary Ann Heap, her mother and then her sister, Jessie Heap with her baby niece, also called Annie Rhodes.

Frank Rhodes, father of Frank, aged two, 1914. He lived at Queen Street. After their marriage Annie and Ernest lived at Mona (late Edward) Street, where Frank senior was born.

Frank Rhodes senior, in front, with his brother Harry, 1930. They are outside their home on Trust Road. The William Sutton Trust housing association built these houses along with those on Sutton Road, both named after the trust. The estate, now one hundred years old, is bounded by Darras, Melland, Mount and Levenshulme Roads and has its estate office on Forber Crescent.

Above left: Irene Walsh and her boyfriend Colin Southworth in the back yard of her home at No. 27, Pollitt Street in the late 1950s. Pollitt Street lay off the north side of Hyde Road near Clowes Street.

Above right: Irene Walsh standing on the cobbled road outside her home at No. 27, Pollitt Street and dressed up for the Whit Walks, in the late 1940s.

Opposite above: Jean Reynolds with her baby daughter Tracy in Buckley Street off Turner Street, in the 1950s.

Opposite below: Jean Reynolds with her daughter Tracy standing in Turner Street at the back of the Labour club, in the 1950s. Turner Street lies between Wellington and Chapman Streets. The Labour club was later moved to Cross Lane.

Colin Southworth with his girlfriend Irene Walsh on his Lambretta, in the late 1950s. Irene lived at No. 27, Pollitt Street, next door to the open front door, which is No. 29.

A group on Hoyland (later William) Street, West Gorton, 1961. The street ran between Great Jackson and Thomas Streets. From the left stand Pete Ford, Pat Beaumont (later Ford), Roy Hough and Alan Crompton. The car is a Ford Popular.

Four

Trade and Work

The ladies of 'Ten Bay' at ICL, 1964. First on the left at the front sits Linda Fidler, next to Alice Clarke. Standing are Marcia, Jean, Beryl and Peggy Melvin. The group worked on printed circuit boards. ICL was based in a tall building on Wenlock Way (late Thomas Street) and Clowes Street (see p.78).

Above: A Whit Walks procession passes eastwards along Hyde Road, West Gorton, 1941. On the left is Elsie Mather (née Beaumont) and the girl on the right is Elsie Beaumont, aged eight. They are just passing Joseph Mottershead's bakery, which later became Edmond's bakery and lay on one corner of Ashmore Street with the Empire Grocery & Provision Co. on the other. On the right is St Mark's church hall and rectory, beyond which were mineral water manufacturer's, Slack & Cox's garage and bottling department.

Left: A group outside Sivori's milk bar at the bottom end of Clowes Street, 1952. From the left at the back stand Stan Booth, Harold Cox and John Commery. At the front are Harold Taylor and Pete Ford. Sivori's had many milk bars around Gorton, including two on Clowes Street and one on Hyde Road (see p.90).

The staff of Woolworth's shop on the south side of Hyde Road, Gorton, in the early 1950s. The shop lay on the corner of Park Avenue next to the Beswick Co-operative and was in a former billiard hall. In the front row, from the left, sit first and second office staff, third, the manager Mr Goddard and fifth, supervisor Terry Hubbard. Second row, sixth, is Margaret Brooks. Back row, fourth, is Helen Jackson (née Carr). The lad in the middle of this row in overalls probably worked in the stockroom, whereas all those in white overalls and hats were in confectionery, selling loose biscuits and sweets.

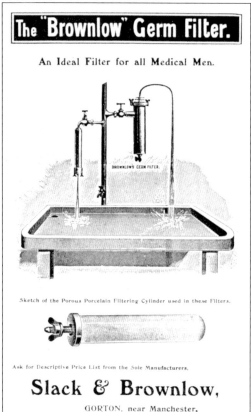

The "Brownlow" Germ Filter.

An Ideal Filter for all Medical Men.

BROWNLOW'S GERM FILTER.

Sketch of the Porous Porcelain Filtering Cylinder used in these Filters.

Ask for Descriptive Price List from the Sole Manufacturers,

Slack & Brownlow,

GORTON, near Manchester.

Above: The rear of Charles Middleton's firm of funeral directors on Hyde Road, West Gorton, 2002. The business stood near the corner of Clowes Street and, although surviving earlier clearances, awaits demolition, like the Junction Hotel, which lay nearby.

Left: An advertisement of 1902 for the 'Brownlow' Germ Filter produced by Slack & Brownlow, originally in Hulme and by the early 1900s on Abbey Hey Lane, Gorton. By the late 1800s they produced a water filter 'warranted to effectually purify river, rain or pipe water free from taste or colour'. The water was passed through a chamber of charcoal, rather like modern water filters and was sold to homes, businesses and shipping, as well as exported. They exhibited this filter at the Great Exhibition in 1851.

The front of the Crown iron works on Malpas and Boundary Streets, West Gorton. To the left lie the offices of the Belle Vue works, where Brayshaw Furnaces and Tools Ltd moved to in 1933, from their works in Hulme, where they had started in around 1890. In 1844 the east side of the works was owned by Higginbottam & Mannock. In around 1970 William Shakeshaft moved in and the firm still operates as PBSI. On the left across the road was the Globe iron works, now the site of a hotel.

A typical 'Super Lopress' furnace installed in aircraft manufacturing firms for the treatment of aero engine parts and produced by Brayshaw Furnaces &Tools Ltd, which operated from the Belle Vue works, West Gorton. The firm closed down in 1966 unable to recruit enough workforce.

The entrance to the yard of the Sirius works of Holden & Brooke & Co. on Haverford (late Heywood) Street, off Clowes Street, West Gorton. The date over the doorway reads 1870 but this firm began life in Salford in 1883 and moved here only in 1897, setting up this maintenance depot. They made water pumps for steam boilers, in particular the Boiler Feed Injector pump.

The yard and buildings of the Sirius works of Holden & Brooke & Co. on Haverford Street. On Thomas Street (later Wenlock Way) in West Gorton was the firm of Frank Pearn & Co., established in 1878. This joined with Holden & Brooke in 1950 and the works there was known as the Pearn works of Holden & Brooke.

Above: The remains of the Imperial brewery off Birch Street, West Gorton, 1983. The brewery has gone now but its attached public house, The Imperial, still stands. Stopford's brewery on Birch Street owned about eighty public houses and was taken over by Walker Holmfray's brewery in 1927, who was in turn bought out by Wilson's in 1949.

Right: The emblem of the Openshaw Brewery Co. of Brook Street, West Gorton, 1892. This large brewery occupied three sides of a square with three storied buildings, which included stables and a cooperage. They moved from Openshaw into the Victora brewery on the banks of the Cornbrook in 1890 and produced mild and bitter ales and porters. By 1897 they supplied 127 public houses but in 1957 they sold out and the site was cleared in 1964.

A letterhead of the firm commonly known as Gorton Tank on Cornwall Street on the border of Openshaw and West Gorton, 1945. The letterhead includes the stamp of the National Scheme for Disabled men, as this was the end of the Second World War. The address on the letter is Gorton but most of the firm lay in Openshaw. They were the running sheds, later railway workshops, of the Sheffield, Ashton and Manchester Railway Company, where Richard Peacock of Beyer Peacock & Co. started as a locomotive superintendant.

The office block of Beyer Peacock & Co. from inside the works looking north with Railway Street on the right and Froxmer Street to the left, in the early 1900s. Richard Peacock left Gorton Tank to join with Henry Robertson and another mechanical engineer from Saxony called Charles Beyer to form this firm in 1854. Designed by Beyer himself, who also built many of the machine tools used there, the works lay on twelve acres beside the railway lines off Gorton Lane.

The yard inside the Gorton Foundry works of Beyer Peacock & Co., 1947. On the left stands Ernest Rhodes. Up to closure in 1966, they had built over 8,000 locomotives and Peacock photographed each one in his lifetime. They built engines to other people's designs and exported many more. During the Second World War they also produced tanks, shells and munitions.

The Southsider in service on the Isle of Man railway system in the early 1980s. This steam engine, produced at the Beyer Peacock company's Gorton foundry in 1894, carries the firm's name plate. In 1890 the firm produced the first electric locomotive together with the firm of Mather & Platt. The Garratt locomotive was another famous product until 1958, through their engineer Garratt who patented it in 1907. Later they also made diesel engines for British Rail.

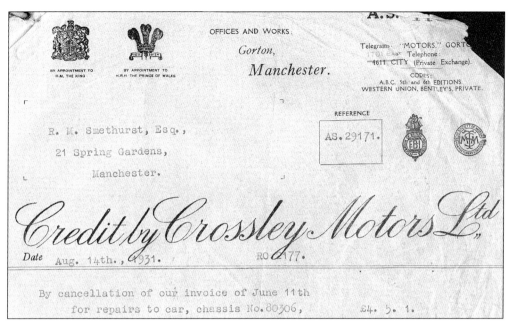

Above: A letterhead of the firm of Crossley Motors Ltd, 1931. William and Frank Crossley's offices and works were on Gorton Lane but their engines were produced in Openshaw. Between 1904 and 1937 they produced expensive, hand-built cars. Then between 1928 and 1958 5,500 motor buses, including the Arrow, were built. 21,000 goods and military vehicles were made between 1914 and 1945.

Right: An advertisement from 1923 for Crossley Motors Ltd. They exported their cars all over the world , including a record crossing of Africa from the Cape to Cairo by two Crossley cars. A Maharajah in Nepal ordered a Canberra Landaulette in 1930 and had it carried piece by piece through the Himalayas to Kathmandu. In 1951 the firm moved to Heaton Chapel and was eventually taken over by Rolls Royce.

Opposite below: The Crescent service station on Reddish Lane, pre-1956. This lay opposite the Bull's Head public house on the right, where the border lies between Reddish, Gorton and Denton. On the left is Mildred Anderson, sister to Vera Bromage, whose father Eric worked at this car showroom.

An advertisement in 1900 for a Chain Tennis model lawn mower designed and produced by Follows & Bate Ltd, engineers of Froxmer Street. Moving here from the city of Manchester in 1890, they produced paint, agricultural and horticultural machinery. They were best known for their side-wheel driven mower, such as the Climax in 1869. With its lower production costs, it was a success, as it was affordable by more people.

An advertisement from the early 1900s by Follows & Bate Ltd for their Pony mower, which was gear-driven and had a front grass box with a simple emptying system. They also designed the Speedwell, which had a canvas grass box at the rear and which cost £1 1s 9d. The firm closed down in 1978.

Five

At Church and School

A class at Peacock Street primary school, in the early 1950s. In the third row from the front, second from the right, sits Linda McGuirk. The school opened in 1928 and closed in 1983 to become a special education centre.

Above: A certificate recording the Holy Baptism of Susan Taylor, daughter of James and Lily, 1946. The baptism took place at All Saints' parish church and was conducted by the Revd Louis. The school preceded the church, being used as a mission church of St James from 1869. The church, consecrated in 1879 and built to a design by J.R. Shaw at a cost of £7,000, was funded by Charles Beyer of Beyer Peacock & Co. (see pp.60-62) for the area's rapidly expanding workforce. Beyer died before completion, leaving £10,000 for the church's construction.

Left: The 48 feet high square tower of All Saints' parish church on Queen's Road, 1963. The foundations of both church and rectory were affected by subsidence. The rectory, nicknamed the 'Rocking Rectory', as it swayed in the wind, was demolished in 1961 and fire in 1963 put paid to plans to rebuild the church. The parish eventually joined first with St Mark's to become Emmanuel and then with St James's, Gorton.

Standard 7 of All Saints' parish church school, 1931. Doris Southern holds the name board. The school preceded the church, opening nearby in 1875 on Queen's Road and being used also as a mission church. It was opened by Charles Beyer of Beyer Peacock & Co. and by the Bishop of Manchester.

A class from All Saints' parish church school, 1946. This first school was destroyed by fire in the late 1960s and a new school was erected on Windicott Close off Gorton Lane near the site of the old one.

Above: The interior of St James's parish church on Church (later Cambert) Lane, in the early 1900s. Probably beginning life as a Chapel of Ease, the original Gorton Chapel was opened in the mid 1500s, being one of only nine in Manchester parish and from 1730 containing an unique chained library. A new Gorton Chapel was built in 1755, often referred to as St Thomas's, and was used as the parish church until demolition in 1871.

Left: The exterior of St James's parish church on Church Lane in the 1980s. The parish of St James's was formed in 1839 and used Gorton Chapel until a new church, designed by G. Shaw, was built in 1871. In 1996 this church joined with Emmanuel (St Mark's and All Saints').

Above: The wedding of Doris and Eddie Scorah at St James's parish church, 1949. The houses on the left are still on Cambert (late Church) Lane and are named by a plaque 'St James's View 1882'.

Right: The wedding of Frank and Ethel Rhodes at St James's church, 1943. Ethel was brought up in Ardwick but Frank was born in 1912 at Edward (later Mona) Street to Ernest and Annie (née Heap) and had a sister Annie (see pp 48-49). In 1912 he was baptised at St James's church, as was his son Frank in 1950.

The demolition of St James's parish church school on Wellington Street, 1976. By 1717 Gorton Chapel had its own school building in the churchyard of St Thomas's on Church Lane. A larger school, known as Gorton Old Endowed school, was built by public subscription in 1783 on the corner of Cross Lane and Wellington Street and was closed in 1905.

Standard 5 of St James's parish church school, 1932. Second row from the back, second from the left is Edith Hicks. In 1838 the Sunday School of St James's church on the corner of Green Lane and Wellington Street became a National Day School and was extended in 1872. In 1976 the school was transferred to new accommodation on Stelling Street.

St. Georges Church, Abbey Hey Lane

Above: The exterior of St George's parish church on Abbey Hey Lane on the corner of Union Street, 1921. A Droylsden Co-operative store was on the opposite corner of Union Street. A mission room preceded this church and lay between Green Fold and Lake Street on Abbey Hey Lane. The parish was formed in 1903 and the original church is part of the parish hall. This second church was erected in 1912.

Right: Four rectors of St Mark's parish church pictured on a postcard sent by Canon Bird Stopford to Mr Williams, the grandfather of Audrey Worthington, 1915.

Left: An interior view of St Mark's church, West Gorton, in the 1960s. This church, designed by Isaac Holden, was consecrated in 1865. It joined with All Saints' parish church to form Emmanuel and the building was eventually demolished in 1974.

Below: The parish church of St Mark's on Clowes Street, West Gorton, in the late 1950s. The Church Lads' brigade of the church march from it on a Whit Walk. The church hall lay on Hyde Road (see p.54).

A class of St Mark's parish church school, 1953. From left to right, back row: Tommy White, Joan Copperswaith, Pauline Tippetts, Sheila Williams, June Haigh, Doris Johnson, Margaret Smith, Christine Haslam, Billy Grimshaw, Mr Brockway (teacher). Second row: Frank Walsh, -?-, Chris Parkinson, -?-, Ian McConnel, Derek Lowndes, Tommy Lamb, Kenny Brooks, Ray Long. Third row: Elsie Frost, Beryl Gunby, Ann Lowndes, Dorothy Hepworth, Joan Broomhead, Ann Bevin, Dinah Knowles, Irene Ogden. Front row: Leslie Baguley, A. Bevin, Walter Carr, Ronnie Coglan, Keith Collier, Alan Wain.

The wedding of Thomas Reynolds and Jean Fidler at St Mark's parish church in March 1954. They were married by Revd Geddis, who is on the right, and their Best Man, Eric Stringer, stands on the left.

A baptismal certificate for Barbara Taylor, sister of Elsie Slockett, from St Philip's parish church, 1935. It includes pictures of the font, as well as the exterior and interior of the church, which was consecrated in 1909 and designed by W.C. Hardisty. The parish was actually formed in 1904 from that of St James's and a mission church was erected, later to become the church hall.

The crowning of the Rose Queen, on the right, of St John's Sunday school and mission church, 1956. On the left is the Rosebud Queen, Barbara Cordwell. In the centre, wearing hoods, are left, Helen Hannan (née McGuirk) and right, Sandra Knight. They are outside the mission church which was at the top of Furnival Road. Taylor Street is to the right (see p.101).

Birch Street Baptist chapel, West Gorton, 1972. The church lay between Blackwin (later Brunswick) and Birch Streets. In 1878 a Baptist church and school were opened on Ainsworth Street to be replaced by this larger building in 1880. They then joined with the Union Baptist chapel on Clowes Street in about 1970 to form the West Gorton Baptist Fellowship, finally joining with Wellington Street Baptists in around 1975.

Gorton United Methodist Free chapel on Hyde Road. Opened in 1903, it replaced a mission church in a school room off Gore Street and was funded by a local Methodist J.H. Crosfield, after whom Crosfield Grove (on the right) is named. Eventually in 1958 it became the central Gorton Methodist chapel and then by 1990 Gorton Evangelical church. A memorial plaque, laid by Titus Laycock for the Sunday school, lies down Crosfield Grove, where the Sunday school is visible.

The Sunday school and schoolroom of Wellington Street Baptist chapel, 1998. This lies behind the site of the chapel, which was built in 1873, replacing their first home across the road, where a Sunday school had existed since 1829. The chapel became the final home for the three Gorton Baptist churches, under the name of the Trinity Baptist church, in around 1975, and after demolition in 2001 awaits rebuilding.

The extension of the Sabbath school rooms of Wellington Street Baptist chapel, 1998. The first schoolroom on this site was opened in 1884 and extended in 1930, funded by various local Baptists, including Mr Doggart who donated £3,000. There are seventeen inscribed stones on the building naming the benefactors, as well as the architects of this extension, Thorpe & Collier of Manchester.

Children of Sacred Heart Roman Catholic church stand in the church grounds in the 1950s. On the right is the original church and on the left the Presbytery, now filled in under the upper storey. The church lies on Levenshulme Road on the corner of Glencastle (late Williams) Road. This original building of 1926 followed a Mission church of 1902 to be itself replaced by the modern church.

The annual school sports day in the grounds of Sacred Heart Roman Catholic church, in the late 1940s. On the left is Vera Bromage (née Anderson) winning the sprint race.

A class from Peacock Street primary school, 1961. From left to right, front row: John Cheffings, Paul Leadbeater, Carl Peel, -?-, Roy Griffiths, Paul Dyer, -?-, Derek France. Second row: Christine Hardman, Diane Bramhall, Georgina Berwick, Eileen Naylor, Mavis Byrom, Anne Harding, Katherine Quirk, Carole Clay, Sylvia Atherton. Third row, standing: G. Jones, D. Graham, -?-, Keith Clayton, Alan McAvoy, Christopher Stubbs, Philip Goulding, John Atherton. Back row: Chris Bowker, Elizabeth Pike, Christine Taylor, Jean Stonier, Jeanette Reid, Sheila Moore, Lesley Slater, Glenis Jones, Les ?

Opposite below: West Gorton Union Baptist chapel on the corner of Clowes and Kelsall Streets, prior to demolition in the mid 1970s. In the background is the tall ICL building (see p. 53). On the right is just visible the chapel's school down Kelsall Street. Built in 1868, this chapel joined first with the Birch Street and then the Wellington Street Baptists to form the Trinity Baptist church at Wellington Street.

A class from Peacock Street primary school, 1953. They are in the playground with Casson Street in the background, where the fair used to be held on the shale area. Third from the left in the middle row is Mavis Oldham.

A class in the yard of Peacock Street primary school in the 1950s. Peacock Street runs behind them, meeting with Gorton Lane on the left. In the front row Peter McClure sits first on the right. In the second row from the left sit, third, Helen McGuirk, fourth, Susan ?, sixth, Gaynor Heap and seventh, Yvonne ? . In the third row stand, sixth, Janet ?, eleventh, Barbara Jones and twelfth, Sammy Davies. In the back row stand sixth, Malcolm ? and seventh, Ivor ?.

A class outside Thomas Street primary school in the early 1960s. On the front row, seventh from the left seated, is Tracy Reynolds. This school was opened as a Board school in 1894.

A class outside Thomas Street primary school, c. 1962. In the back row stands Tracy Reynolds fourth from the left. The road was changed to Wenlock Way and so was the school's name but it was closed in 1978.

The prefects of Ryder Brow secondary school at Christmas, 1957. From left to right, front: David Maclin, Anne Pullen, Ronnie Woodcock, Mr Lloyd Jones (head teacher), Linda McGuirk, David Higgins, Brenda Vernon. Middle row: Val Cryer, Brian Muyton, Margaret Lancaster, Paul Ray, Wilfred Newman, David Thornley, Glo Fletcher, Jack Darlington Anne Rainford. Back row: Joy Walker, Frank Smith, Jaqueline Ellershaw, Phillip Palmer, Jean Phythian, Gordon Flevil, Jean Hicks.

Opposite below: Pupils of Ryder Brow secondary school in the 1950s. From the left in the front row sit, fifth, Ronnie Woodcock and, sixth, Frank Smith. In the second row sit, second, Linda McGuirk and sixth, Anne Pullen. In the third row stand, first, Val Cryer, second, Jack Darlington and last, the head teacher, Mr Lloyd Jones. In the back row stands, first, Jean Hicks.

Pupils of Ryder Brow seconday school in the 1950s. The school was opened in 1952 and in 1967 became the lower school of Spurley Hey high school, with Spurley Hey secondary school becoming the upper school.

Pupils of Ryder Brow secondary school in the 1950s. They are standing in the playground, which adjoined that of Old Hall Drive primary school. From the left in the front row sit, fourth, the head teacher, Mr Lloyd Jones, fifth, June Faulkner and, seventh, Margaret White. In the middle row stand, second, Alan Jones and, fourth, Barry ? In the back row stand, third, Helen McGuirk, fourth, Linda Metcalf and, sixth, Sandra Ward.

A netball team from Ryder Brow secondary school in the 1950s. In the front rows sits, fourth from the left, Helen McGuirk and in the back row stands, first, Joyce Collins.

A netball team from Ryder Brow secondary school in the 1950s. On the front row, second from the left, sits Helen McGuirk and on the back row, third, stands Mary Potts.

A class in Old Hall Drive primary school, 1960. From left to right, back row: John McIntyre, Philip Kelly, Gerald Scruton, Susan Gunson, opposite -?-. In front of them sit Frank Rhodes, Keith Jones and Kenneth Glover, opposite Barry Duffy and David Shanks. At the back of the room stand Margaret Brookes and -?-. On the right sit Brian Nuttall and Glynis Jones with David Talbot and Reginald Bethell standing behind them.

A class at Old Hall Drive primary school, 1959/60. Left to right, front: Barry Duffy, Tony Wyatt, Frank Minshull, Alan Lowe, Alan Nicholls, David? Nicholls, David Kirk, Howard Gittens, David Talbot, Thomas Cox. Second row: Susan Grandin, -?-, Susan Barlow, -?-, -?-, Odetta Pratico, -?-, Irene Greenhalgh, -?-, Margaret Brooks. Third row: Michael Overend, David Walker, Chris Howe, David -?-, Frank Rhodes, Peter Scholes? , Paul Bowling, Michael Grady, Robert Kingsley, Raymond Millbanks, David Livingstone. Back row: Alan Gough, -?-, Pauline Owen, -?-, Caroline Oliver, Edith Barber, Susan Lomas, -?-, Pauline Locke, Tony Hodnett. The school was opened in 1914 for all ages and the seniors transferred to Spurley Hey secondary school in 1932.

Six

Special Events and Leisure Activities

Gathering for the Whit Walk procession on Gorton Lane in the early 1900s. On the left is just visible St James's parish church, on the corner of Wellington Street and Gorton Lane, near the tram. On the right behind the crowd lies St James's church school. In the centre is the garage of Lamb's haulage firm, separated from the school by Green Lane. Just off the right hand bottom corner was the Congregational chapel.

VE Day street party for the adults of Furnival Road, off Taylor Street, West Gorton, 1946. Among those on the left-hand side are Mrs Robinson, Mrs Booth, Mrs Robinson (snr), Mrs Cordwell, Mrs Craven, Mrs Morris and Mrs Ritson. At the top of the table is Mr Booth, in charge of the teapot. Among those on the right are Mrs Mullen, Mrs Allen, Mrs McGuirk, Mrs Hanson and Mrs Collins.

Above: VE Day street party for the children of Furnival Road, off Taylor Street, West Gorton, 1946. On the left stand Mrs Craven, Mrs Cordwell, Mrs Collins and Mrs Morris, with Mrs Fox on the right.

Right: A VE Day party on Green Street, parallel with Queen's Road near Gorton Park, 1945.

A Whit Walk procession on Clowes Street in West Gorton in the 1960s. They are just passing Sivori's milkbar on the corner of Hardy Street and behind them lies the turning into Gregory Street. Between the two streets in 1965 lay Sivori's, the long frontage of a chemist's, a newsagent's and then a hairdresser's shop. Nearby lay the Conway cinema on Clowes Street.

The Sunday School of St Mark's parish church, West Gorton, taking part in a Whit Walk, 1956. In the second row of boys are Frank Torr, David Sinclair and Fred Torr on the right. Second from the right is Brenda Beaumont. They are just passing the Justice Birch public house on the north side of Hyde Road. Next door on the left is W. Hart's dental practice with St Mark's Ward Conservative Association opposite. Elland Street lies to the left and Deepdene Street to the right.

Opposite below: A Whit Walk procession on Hyde Road near the Horse Shoe Inn in the 1950s. In 1881 William Turnell was landlord. The inn is at the far end of the row of shops on the left.

Choir girls from St Mark's church in procession along Clowes Street in West Gorton on a Whit Walk, 1952. From the left are Brenda Beaumont, Elsie Pugh, Brenda's twin Pat and Pauline and Barbara Fairfield. Behind Elsie is Pauline Tippetts.

A Whit Walk procession along Hyde Road, West Gorton, 1968. At the front from the left are the children, Beverley Hunt, Paula Ford and Janice Sinclair of St Mark's church. They are walking eastwards and just passing Deepdene (late Hampden) Street with Joe's café on the left-hand corner and the Harrington Inn on the other, where May and Stan Dorrington were the landlords at that time. The café was a gentlemen's hairdresser's in 1965.

Members of the Church Lads' brigade from St Mark's church taking part in a Whit Walk along the north side of Hyde Road in the 1950s. They are marching eastwards and have just passed Robert Street where lies the Horse Shoe Inn, a Bell & Co. public house. Next door in 1965 were Stott & Browne's hardware shop, Brough's draper's, Bannister's fried fish shop and Wilson's bakery with Jones' radio, Noblett's florist's and then Draba's newsagent's shops on the corner of Beaumaris Street, just off the photograph.

Members of St Mark's Church Lads' brigade marching along Hyde Road, West Gorton, in the 1950s. In the distance is West Gorton Wesleyan Methodist chapel, which was built in 1873 and closed in 1969.

Members of the Church Lads' brigade of St Mark's church walk along Clowes Street away from Gorton Lane towards Hyde Road in the 1950s. On the right, beyond Graveney (later George) Street, lies the Co-operative shop next to a tram office and followed by Sivori's milk bar. In 1965 the row of shops on the left began by Graveney Street with Willis' ladies wear, Thomson's butchers, Black's hardware store and Arrowsmith's cycle shop.

Taking part in a Whit Walk on Church Lane in the 1950s are children from St James's parish church. Sheila Moore stands third from the left.

Children from St James's parish church assemble for a Whit Walk near their church on Church (later Cambert) Lane, 1950. Robert Rhodes, aged five, stands third from the left.

Children from St James's parish church on a Whit Walk, 1930. They are standing outside the Midland Hotel on Hyde Road near Belle Vue. The chimney belongs to Chatsworth Mills on Williams Road, where Robert Williams & Sons were silk finishers.

Children from All Saints' parish church walking along Queen's Road on their Whit Walk, marching from Hyde Road up the side of Gorton Park on the right, 1939. Second and third from the right, front, are Barbara and Elsie Taylor.

The children of All Saints' parish church proceed from the church grounds on their Whit Walk, 1939. In the third pair are Elsie Slockett (née Taylor) and her sister Barbara on the right, both wearing ribbons.

The banner of the Sunday School of Crossley Street Mission chapel is carried along Hyde Road, 1946. Second from left in the procession is Elsie Slockett (née Taylor) and they are near the Cosmo cinema on Wellington Street.

Children take part in a Whit Walk along Queen's Road, 1939. In the procession are Christine Taylor, Sylvia Williams, Barbara Taylor and Nelly Griffin. They are walking towards Hyde Road with Gorton Park on the left. With them is the banner of Gore Street Mission chapel.

Children dressed in their new clothes, ready for a Whit Walk, 1955. It was customary to visit neighbours and family to be admired and rewarded with small change. At the back stand from the left Arthur Tippetts and Fred Torr. In front stand Frank Torr and David Sinclair. They are outside their great grandmother's house on Great Jackson (later Donnison) Street. David was her great great grandson.

Members of the 9th Gorton Gore Street Mission church guide company on Church (later Cambert) Lane facing the direction of Hyde Road, in the 1950s. In the centre is Linda McGuirk. The banner behind them belongs to Wellington Street Sunday school Methodist church. Behind them also lies the turning to Taylor Street with a beer seller on its far corner and a private house on its other.

A Whit Walks procession from St John's Mission church, on Chapman Street in the 1950s. On the right is J.W. Strafford builder's yard on the corner of Stelling (late Croft) Street with Ellis's petrol station next door.

The May Queen, Anne Pullen, with her Maid of Honour Linda McGuirk, taking part in a Whit Walk on Taylor Street in the 1950s. Taylor Street leads to Gorton Lane to the left and Church Lane to the right. Behind them lies Poplar Street with Knowle's off licence and grocer's shop on the right and Knight's greengrocer's on the left. Reg and Kay Knight stand in front of their shop with their assistant, Edith McGuirk, standing between them.

The May Queen, Maureen Ritson, of St John's Mission chapel takes part in the Whit Walks, in the early 1950s. Helen McGuirk is on the far right.

Children lining up for a Whit Walk on Taylor Street in the 1950s. From the left stand Barbara Lucas, Helen McGuirk, Carol Spencer, Rita ?, -?-, -?- and Barbara Cordwell. Knowle's off licence and grocery shop lies on the left on the corner of Poplar Street.

Members of St John's Mission church proceed in a Whit Walk along Chapman Street in the 1950s. Behind the banner is the builder's yard of J.W. Strafford on the corner of Stelling Street. Strafford built the Kings' Hall at Belle Vue and the Debdale housing estate.

The Rose Queen, Anne Pullen, aged fourteen, is crowned on the stage at St John's Mission church for the year 1956/57. The Mission lay at the top of Furnival Road off Taylor Street. It appears on a map of 1905 but the whole area was cleared by 1965 (see p.75).

Members of the Church Lads' brigade of St Mark's parish church, West Gorton, 1931. On the front row, seated seventh from the left, is the minister Revd Newall, ninth is Captain Harry Sidebottom, tenth, Harry Jones. In the second row standing third from the left is Cyril Eastwood, fourth, Fred Downs and twentieth, Jack Eastwood. In the third row stands, first, Norman Symister and in the back row, second, is Harry Doodry and, fourth, Clifford Eastwood. The company was formed in 1907 when thirty boys enrolled.

Members of Gorton Philharmonic Society pose in front of the Indian Temple and Grotto at Belle Vue in the early 1900s. The society had met at a variety of venues in Reddish and Gorton since its foundation in 1854. John Jennison of Belle Vue saw the opportunity of having them play there and so began the 'open rehearsals', which were in fact free concerts and which continued until 1977.

The cast of a pantomime on the stage of Gorton Congregational church in the 1940s. Lillian Southern is second from the right in the far back row. 'Gorton Congo', as the church on Church Lane was affectionately called, was opened in 1883 and extended in 1905. It became Gorton United Reformed church but was eventually demolished. Another small Congregational chapel also existed on Knutsford Road.

Members of the Church Lads' brigade of St Mark's church, West Gorton, pass by the Corona cinema on Birch Street off Hyde Road in the late 1950s. By then the cinema was for let or for sale. It began life in 1915 as a cinema which closed down in 1958 and then became the Southern Sporting club.

The shell of the Savoy picture house on Savoy Street, which stood at the corner of Donnison and Savoy Streets off Hyde Road, West Gorton, 1991. In the background is the tower of St Benedict's church in Ardwick, as Savoy Street lay near the border of West Gorton and Ardwick. Exits from the cinema were on Great Jackson and St Anne Streets.

Members of the cubs and scouts of Gorton Congregational church in the late 1940s. They are posing outside their church, which lay on Church Lane. Their leader, Doris Southern, is on the right by the flag.

Members of the Girl Guides of Gorton Congregational church standing in procession on a Whit Walk in the 1930s.

Members of the Cub Scouts of Gorton Congregational church posing outside their church on Church Lane in the 1950s. Their neckerchieves were green.

Uniformed organizations take part in a Whit Walk in the 1950s. Their leader Doris Southern is next to the flag in the front. They are from Gorton Congregational church and are passing St James's parish church on Church Lane. They are just marching by Kenyon House (see p. 39), which lay opposite the old Gorton library and on the left, between the trees, St James's school is visible.

Busmen from Hyde Road bus depot on a works outing at the Midland Hotel on Hyde Road in the 1950s. In 1881 the landlady was Mary Cheetham. The Midland was bought by the Jennison family of Belle Vue pleasure gardens in 1887 and sold to the Openshaw Brewery Co. in 1931. It now stands empty.

Members of the Girl Guides of St Mark's church, West Gorton, on a week's camp at Conway, North Wales, 1950. From the left in the third row from the front are, second, Jean Alexander, third, Captain Scott and, fifth, Pauline Tippetts. In the second row are, first, Pat Beaumont (twin) and, second, Elsie Pugh. In the front row are, first, Linda Yarwood, second, Brenda Beaumont (twin), third, Ellen Grimshaw and, fourth, Barbara O'Neill.

Pupils from St Mark's school, West Gorton, on a day's outing to Charlesworth in Derbyshire, 1952. From the left are -?-, Arthur Latham, Ian McConnel, Vivien O'Brien, Joan Broomhead, Brenda Beaumont, Beryl Gunby, Jean Lowe and Irene Ogden.

The Vulcan public house on Gorton Lane, 1993. This was named from the vibration caused by the steam hammer in the nearby works of Beyer Peacock & Co. (see pp.60-62). The foundry building is on the left and Peacock Close on the right. Belonging in the 1870s to Stopford's brewery, it was let to Walker Homfray's brewery by the Palatine Bottling Co. in 1937 and finally taken over by Wilson's in 1968.

The Suburban Hotel public house on Cross (later Gorton-cross) Street in the 1960s. The public house belonged to John W. Lees brewery in the 1870s and later to Bushells. It was home to Gorton cycling club and boasted a concert room. These rows of shops were all cleared away in 1980.

The Duke of York public house on Cross Lane with Roxborough Street on the right, in the 1970s. In the 1870s this was a Clement Wallwork brewery public house, becoming part of Edward Issott's in 1888 and later transferring to Boddington's brewery.

The Plough Inn on Hyde Road with Wellington Street separating it from the bank on the right in the early 1900s. The public house, almost unchanged today, still possesses its cobbled front, where horse-drawn carts, taking goods to and from the city, would park and where Whit Walk marchers assemble. Originally a Holt's public house, it passed to Bell & Co. and later to Robinson's brewery. Here too was the side toll bar in 1851 of the turnpiked Gorton Old Road.

The White Bear Inn on the north side of Hyde Road, West Gorton, in the 1930s. The Salford based Groves & Whitnall brewery had this public house in the 1870s, when Mordecai Smith was landlord from 1872 until 1905. The leasehold was taken over by Walker Holmfray brewery in 1949. On the left lies Kinley Street with the Gorton Villa public house on the street's opposite corner. On the right in 1965 were a greengrocer's and jewellery shops next to Pollitt Street.

Above: The Rose of England public house on Cross Street, 1972. Here is the side view on Gore (later Gorelan) Street. It appears in the licensing records for 1872 and was a Greenall Whitney brewery house.

Right: The side view of the Vale Cottage public house as seen from the nearby Lord Nelson public house in Fox Fold, in the 1950s. The Vale Cottage is tucked away on Croft Bank and fronts the Gore Brook. Wilson's brewery took this public house over from Henry Cordwell & Co. in 1899.

Opposite below: The Junction Hotel on Hyde Road with Clowes Street on the right, West Gorton, in the 1970s. It used to have a board across its top declaring it a Chester's brewery public house, after they purchased it in 1899. In 1881 the landlord was Thomas Platt and in 1905 Albert Griffiths. It was demolished in 2001. Visible on the right is the firm of Holden and Brooke (see p.58).

Above: The Rock Inn public house on Hyde Road, West Gorton, in the 1970s. Licensed in 1868, in the 1870s it was an Empress brewery house with a board along the top declaring this. In 1881 Dracus Collins was beerhouse keeper there. To the left is Boundary Street and on its right used to be cottages.

Right: The former public house Live and Let Live on Belle Vue Street with Blackwin (later Brunswick) Street off to the right. Licensed in 1864, in the 1870s it was a P. Walker brewery house. By the 1960s it became the British Legion Comrades' club.

Opposite below: The Victoria Inn on Hyde Road, West Gorton, 1989. Originally this public house had four cottages attached on the left and two more around the corner on Fenton Street, beyond its archway into its yard. Licensed in 1865, Chesters purchased it in 1888, plus the six cottages, from John Battersby of the Wellington brewery, Bradford, and erected its signboard along the top of the public house. On the right is Belle Vue works (see p.57).

The Brunswick Inn public house on Belle Vue Street. Brunswick (late Blackwin) Street leads off to the left. This lay on the opposite corner to the Live and Let Live public house and, licensed by 1861 when Robert Hough was the landlord, it was an Openshaw brewery house from the 1870s.

The Unicorn Inn on Hyde Road, West Gorton, 1990. Licensed in 1866, it became a Boddington's brewery public house in the 1870s. In 1881 Sarah Clough was a beer retailer there. The cottages and shops adjoining it were demolished.

The Travellers' Call on Hyde Road, West Gorton, 1980. This public house was licensed by 1879 and belonged to the Openshaw brewery. In 1881 Mavis Worsman was the beer house keeper there. In 1903 it was purchased by Hyde's Anvil.

The Steelwork's Tavern on the corner of Gorton Lane and Preston Street, 1993. This public house was purchased by Chesters brewery in 1934. There used to be a row of terraced houses attached to it on the left.

The Lake Hotel on the corner of Hyde Road and Kirkmanshulme Lane on the left, in the 1980s. Opened in 1876, it belonged to the Jennison family, who owned Belle Vue, where they had their own brewery. An entrance into these pleasure gardens lay just at the side of the hotel (see p. 17). The Great Lake, from which it derives its name, has long been drained and in 1989, as a Burtonwood's house, it was closed and later demolished. The last landlady of Belle Vue Lakes, as it was then named, was called Yads.

The Beehive public house on the corner of Gorelan (late Gore) and Hopefield (late Hope) Streets, 1972. It was originally owned by Flatterley of Longsight and the landlord was Ellis Green. It later passed to Hyde's Queen's brewery in the 1870s. In 1974 it was compulsorily purchased and demolished as part of a clearance area.

The Cheshire Hunt on Hyde Road, 1986. Licensed by 1855, in 1861 James Brooks was the landlord. It became a Wilson's brewery house in 1899 after belonging to Henry Cardwell and contained a billiard, music and dance rooms. It still stands but no longer functions as a public house.

The Birch Arms, an Openshaw brewery house, on Gorton Lane and Belle Vue Street, West Gorton in the early 1960s. Next door lie the Brook House flats, demolished in the late 1970s and originally the site of the Yorkshire Hotel (see pp 43-44). Beyond them, on the junction of Gorton Lane, Belle Vue and Clowes Streets, is West Gorton library with its distinctive clock tower, which was closed down in 1960 and also demolished.

The rear of the Birch Arms on Gorton Lane, c. 1934.

Above: The Horse Shoe Inn on Hyde Road, West Gorton, 1989. On the left is Robert Street and on the right once lay a row of shops ending at Beaumaris Street (see pp. 90, 93). Licensed by 1864, this was a Bell & Co. brewery public house in the 1870s. It held a dance and music licence and was demolished as part of a clearance programme along Hyde Road in the 1970s.

Left: The Gorton Arms on the corner of Belle Vue and Clowes Street in the 1990s. Originally called the Gorton Brook Hotel, it was rebuilt in 1929 and included a dance room upstairs. In 1937 it was let by the Palatine Bottling Co. to Walker Holmfray's brewery, it then became a Stopford's house and passed to Wilson's in 1968. In November 2001 a JCB smashed into the rear of the public house rendering it unsafe and its future uncertain.

Above: The rush cart turning away from Hyde Road, 1989. The cart was traditionally built at Fox Fold behind the Lord Nelson public house. Gorton Silver band preceded the cart, which was accompanied by Gorton Morris men as well as Morris men from many other areas. The route in recent years began at Chapman Street, along Stelling Street to the Angel Inn on Wellington Street. They next made for the Suburban Hotel on Garratt Way, marched along Hyde Road, Wellington Street and Cross Street and finished at the Royal Oak.

Right: Gorton rush cart on Chapman Street, 1989. Decorating a rush cart with garlands, rushes and silver plate was first recorded in 1780 in Gorton and last in 1874. Each September the parish church of Gorton Chapel (later St James) had its rush carpeting renewed and the church decorated with rushes. The Rushbearing custom was revived in 1980 for a while by Gorton Morris men but has now been abandoned again.

The Hicks family, who emigrated via Liverpool to Canada to begin a new life in 1927. They sailed on the *Mount Stephen* of the Canada Pacific Rockies line. The sons are Stanley, Ossie, Leonard and Bill with daughters Edna and Edith. In the centre are their father Benjamin and mother Bertha. Benjamin was a miner from South Wales but his wife Bertha came from Gorton. They stayed in Canada for four and a half years and then returned in 1931 and lived on Ryder Brow.

The wedding reception of Margaret and Jim Earley inside Gorton Conservative club on Gorton Lane, March 1964. They were married at St James's church. Seated from the left are Ethel and Frank Rhodes with their son Frank behind them, Jean and Jack Williams with their daughter Lynn, Annie Cornes and Annie and Ernest Hendry. The club backed onto Cambert Lane near Gorton library. The original club was opposite Gorton Park on the east side of Belle Vue Street opposite Grafton Street, on the corner of Blackwin Street, in the early 1900s.

Seven
Gorton Monastery

Gorton Monastery on Gorton Lane, prior to partial demolition and vandalism, in the early 1970s. The full view of the monastery site shows the front entrance to the church of St Francis of Assisi on the left, next to the Franciscan friary, enclosing cloisters. In 1989 the monks departed leaving the complex to be turned into apartments. The project did not materialise and the buildings were vandalised and left derelict. Plans now in action should see the whole complex restored and used for community purposes.

The altar of the Blessed John Forest, martyr, in the early 1900s. This was the last altar to be built in the monastery and was funded by Richard Holden, a Syndic of the friary and a great benefactor. The high altar of Bath stone was dedicated first in 1885 and, like the other altars, was designed by Peter Paul, the younger brother of Edward Welby Pugin, the architect. Other side altars were set up to the Sacred Heart in 1893 and to St Anthony in 1891.

A view of the monastery church from Gorton Lane, in the early 1900s. These fine buildings were designed by Edward Welby Pugin, son of Augustus Pugin, and the church was built during 1866 to 1872 and the rest by 1867. The spire was added to mark the Golden Jubilee in 1911 and rises 80 feet above the roof, supported by three 90 feet high flying buttresses.

Above: The back of the friary, now derelict. The monks built quarters for themselves around three sides of cloisters, with the monastery church forming the fourth side. The front façade of the friary was pulled down in the 1970s, as it was in poor condition. There were also two schools and a hall nearby.

Left: The rear of the complex, now derelict. In the background is the west end of the monastery church where the chancel and high altar lie. On the left is the back section of the friary.

An angel inside the monastery church. An array of angels decorated the walls of the nave, with one angel lying above each column at the foot of a saint. There were twelve saints, they are currently in storage awaiting restoration. The angels have survived in situ.

A detail of the painted walls of the chancel. This is an apse in shape and its painted walls and fine stained glass, depicting the lives of St Francis, St Clare and St Louise, make a fine back-drop for the high altar.

Colin Southworth with his bride Irene Walsh and Father Oliver, who married them at the monastery church, in September 1961. They are standing outside the front of the monastery near the steps by the gate to the infants' school.

Irene Walsh with her uncle Alfred Lee, on her way into the monastery church to marry Colin Southworth, 1961. Behind them is Gorton Lane with the tower of All Saints' parish church in the background. The whole area was cleared in the 1970s and All Saints' church was burned down in 1963 (see p. 66-67).

A Whit Walk from the monastery church in 1950. The monks are seen walking along Queen's Road by Gorton Park.

Julie Southworth in her veil ready for her confirmation at the monastery church in the late 1960s. She is standing on Newton Street, where she lived at No. 47. The lady on the left is Mrs Lamb, with her granddaughter, outside No. 49.

A class from St Francis's girls' school, *c.* 1948. On the front row second from the right sits Irene Walsh. The boys' school existed from 1866 and the girls' had their own building from 1874. By the 1970s both schools were closed.

A class from St Francis's school, 1929.

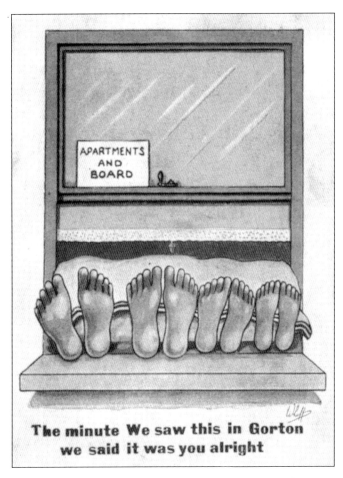

A comic postcard posted from Gorton in about 1912. This was a stock picture, which could have any town's name printed on it.

Acknowledgements

We should like to thank the following organizations and individuals for giving permission for their photographs to be included in this book. We have tried to locate everyone and apologise if anyone has been omitted: Reg and Bet Baguley, Colin Brierley, Vera Bromage, R. Allan Crockford, Mrs Cullen, the late Mrs Fitzgerald, Pat and Peter Ford, Gorton Library and Ken Lilley, Tony and Helen Hannan, Eddie Harris, Mrs Hawkins, the late Stan Horritt, Margaret Johnson, Jim Kind, Marie Koudellas, Dorothy Lord, the *Manchester Evening News*, Sheila Moore, Margaret O'Connor, Thomas Reynolds, Robert Rhodes, Brian Selby, Elsie Slockett, Doris and Lillian Southern, Irene and Colin Southworth, Margaret Williams, Lesley and Audrey Worthington, and Colin Wyatt.

We should also like to thank Barbara Barraclough, as she retires from the Library Service, for her contribution to local history in Gorton over many years.